W9-ABC-728

SHOCKWAVE
SCIENCE

The Water Planet

Library of Congress Cataloging-in-Publication Data

Schmauss, Judy Kentor.
  The Water planet / by Judy Kentor Schmauss.
      p. cm. -- (Shockwave)
  Includes index.
  ISBN 10: 0-531-17795-5 (lib. bdg)
  ISBN 13: 978-0-531-17795-2 (lib. bdg)
  ISBN 10: 0-531-18793-4 (pbk)
  ISBN 13: 978-0-531-18793-7 (pbk)

1. Water--Juvenile literature. I. Title. II. Series.
  GB662.3.S34 2007
  551.46--dc22

2007012233

Published in 2008 by Children's Press, an imprint of Scholastic Inc.,
557 Broadway, New York, New York 10012
www.scholastic.com

SCHOLASTIC, CHILDREN'S PRESS, and associated logos are trademarks
and/or registered trademarks of Scholastic Inc.

08 09 10 11 12 13 14 15 16
10 9 8 7 6 5 4 3 2 1

Printed in China through Colorcraft Ltd., Hong Kong

Author: Judy Kentor Schmauss
Educational Consultant: Ian Morrison
Editor: Jennifer Murray
Designer: Juliet Hughes
Photo Researcher: Jamshed Mistry

Photographs by: BigStockPhoto.com (liner, p. 14); **Brady Doak** (p. 3; divers, pp. 20–21;
divers, pp. 24–25, 34); **Brand X Pictures** (fish, bottom p. 31); **Getty Images** (cover; p. 17;
submersible, pp. 20–21; giant squid, p. 22; netted fish, pp. 32–33); **Hank F. Seidel,
Texas A&M University Oceanography Department/Ashanti Johnson Pyrtle, University
of South Florida College of Marine Science** (Ashanti Pyrtle at work, p. 29); **Jennifer
and Brian Lupton** (teenagers, pp. 32–33); **Photolibrary** (turtle, p. 14; squid tentacles
close-up, p. 22); **Stock.Xchng** (snorkels, microscope, barometer, p. 25); **Stockxpert**
(garbage, ocean liner, pp. 26–27); **Tranz: Corbis** (p. 7; pp. 8–9; turtle, background waves,
pp. 12–13; background water, gulf stream, pp. 14–15; pp. 18–19; Steve O'Shea and giant
squid, p. 23; beach litter, pp. 26–27); **Rex Features** (nuclear power plant, pp. 28–29)

The publisher would like to thank Brady Doak for the use of his photo collection.

All illustrations and other photographs © Weldon Owen Education Inc.

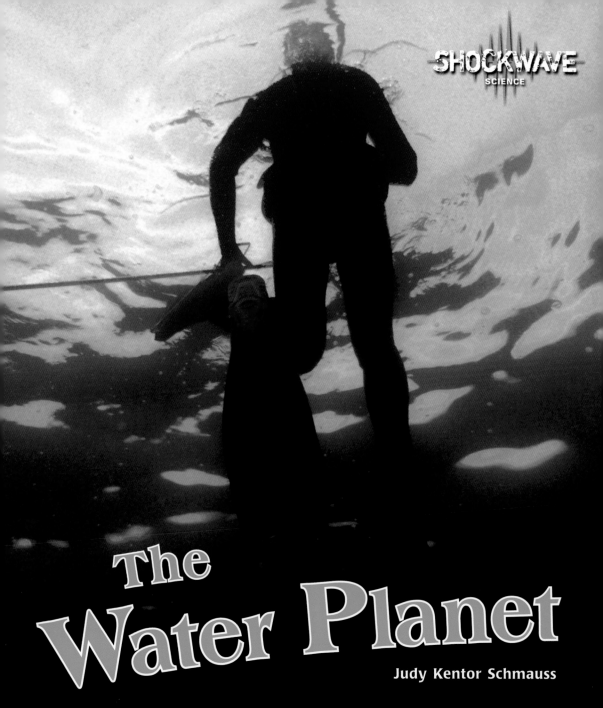

SHOCKWAVE
SCIENCE

The Water Planet

Judy Kentor Schmauss

children's press®

An imprint of Scholastic Inc.
NEW YORK • TORONTO • LONDON • AUCKLAND • SYDNEY
MEXICO CITY • NEW DELHI • HONG KONG
DANBURY, CONNECTICUT

CHECK THESE OUT!

SHOCKER

Stuff to Shock,
Surprise, and
Amaze You

Quick Recaps
and Notable
Notes

Word Stunners
and Other Oddities

?

The Heads-Up
on Expert Reading

Links to More
Information

CONTENTS

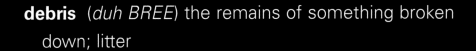

debris (*duh BREE*) the remains of something broken down; litter

evaporate (*ee VAP uh rate*) to change from a liquid into a vapor, or gas

hydrothermal vent a crack or hole in the surface of the land or ocean floor through which hot water shoots up

oceanographer a scientist who studies the oceans and the things that live in the oceans

organism (*OR guh niz uhm*) a living thing

submersible (*sub MUR si bul*) a small underwater craft that is usually used for deep-sea study

trench a valley in the ocean

· ·

For additional vocabulary, see Glossary on page 34.

In the word *submersible*, *sub* means "under," and *mer* is the French word for "sea" or "ocean." Other words that use *sub* or *mer* are *submerge*, *substandard*, and *mermaid*.

Oceans cover about 71 percent of the earth's surface. They are home to a huge range of plant and animal life. Oceans affect the land and the climate. New technology has been developed to explore ocean depths. People are learning more about the oceans and underwater life.

You probably know that oceans are salty. Did you know that oceans are also the source of about 97 percent of the fresh water that falls to the earth? When the oceans absorb heat from the sun, water **evaporates**. Salt is left behind. As the water evaporates, it becomes water vapor in the air. It then **condenses** back into tiny drops of water or pieces of ice. These make up clouds. Eventually, the water falls as rain or snow. Much of this water returns to the oceans. This process is called the water cycle.

1. Oceans absorb heat from the sun.

The water cycle reminds me of another cycle I know about – the life cycle of the butterfly. In both cycles, there is no real starting or finishing point. I am guessing that all cycles may be like this.

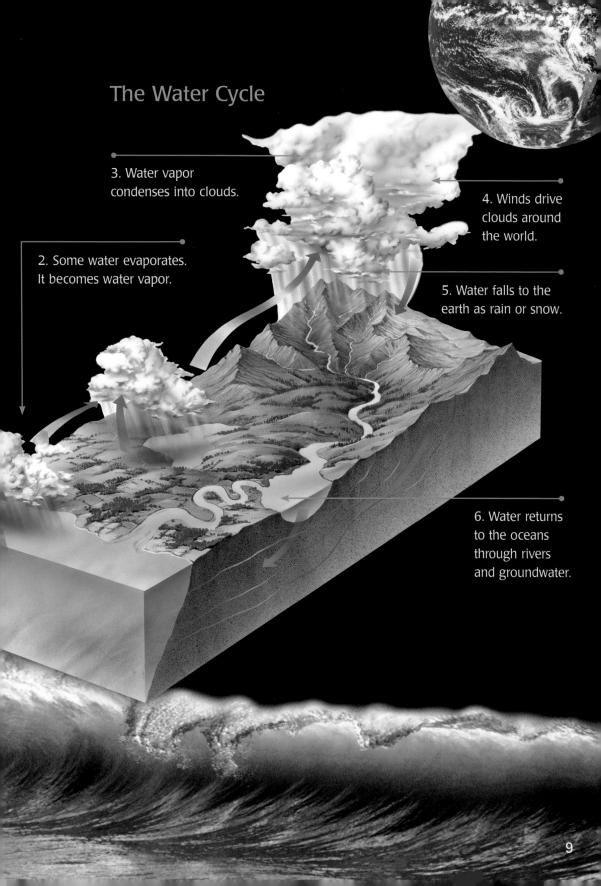

The Water Cycle

3. Water vapor condenses into clouds.

4. Winds drive clouds around the world.

2. Some water evaporates. It becomes water vapor.

5. Water falls to the earth as rain or snow.

6. Water returns to the oceans through rivers and groundwater.

Earth's Oceans

Scientists believe that 200 million years ago, the earth's surface looked very different from the way it looks today. There were no separate **continents**. There was one huge piece of land, which scientists call Pangaea. The rest of the earth was covered by a great ocean, which is called Panthalassa.

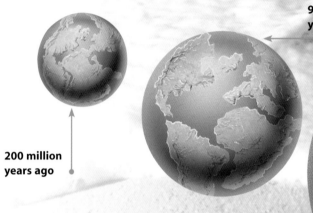

90 million
years ago

200 million
years ago

Present
day

Then Pangaea broke up into several pieces. These began to drift apart. They formed the seven continents that we know today. The water between the continents is connected, but we think of it as five separate oceans. The oceans are still changing shape. Every year, the Atlantic Ocean gets wider by a few inches.

Of course, you know that the earth is more or less spherical. But imagine that the planet was totally flat and that the oceans were evenly spread out. If this were the case, the water would be about two miles deep everywhere!

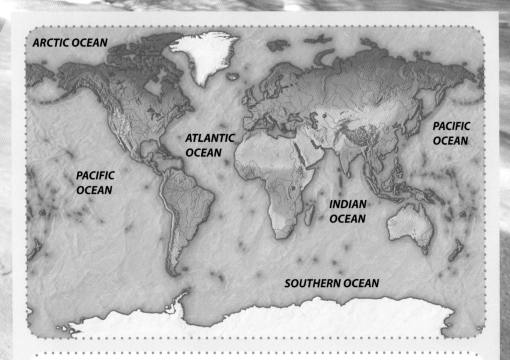

NAME OF OCEAN	HOW BIG IT IS	AVERAGE DEPTH
Pacific Ocean	62,000,000 square miles	14,215 feet
Atlantic Ocean	31,500,000 square miles	12,800 feet
Indian Ocean	27,400,000 square miles	13,000 feet
Southern Ocean	7,800,000 square miles	14,000 feet
Arctic Ocean	5,300,000 square miles	3,900 feet

Ocean Movement

The earth's oceans are constantly moving. Tides go in and out. There are high tides and low tides. Tides are the **ebb** and **flow** of the ocean. The pull of **gravity** from the moon affects the part of Earth nearest to it. Gravity tugs at the ocean, causing the water to rise. As the earth spins, different parts of the oceans rise and fall.

Changing Tides

The pull of gravity from both the sun and the moon affects the tides. The pull of gravity from the sun is weaker. This is because the sun is so far away. The biggest tides occur when the sun and moon are pulling in the same direction. These are called spring tides.

Spring Tides

When the sun and moon are pulling at right angles to each other, the high tides are at their lowest. These are called neap tides.

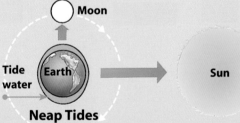

Neap Tides

SHOCKER

The highest tides in the world are in the Bay of Fundy in Canada. The difference between high and low tide is nearly 52 feet!

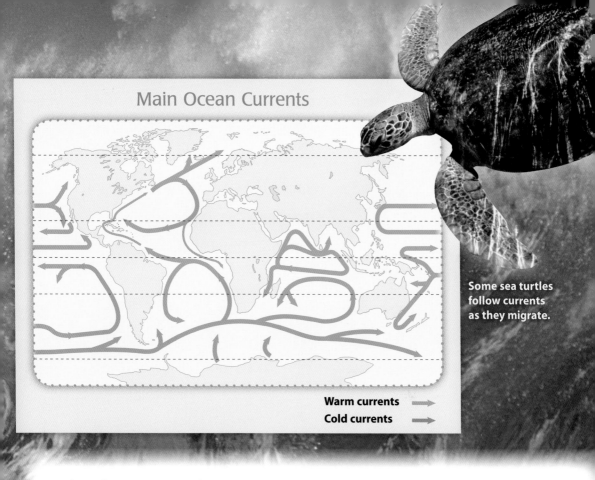

Main Ocean Currents

Some sea turtles follow currents as they migrate.

Warm currents →
Cold currents →

Other things that make the oceans move include **currents**. Currents stir up minerals. They can carry marine plants and animals all around the world. There are different kinds of currents. Some are surface currents, and some are deep under water.

Surface currents are caused by the wind. The wind pushes the water at the top of the ocean. This creates currents of moving water that are about 330 feet deep. The wind also creates waves.

Duck Voyages!

In 1992, about 29,000 rubber ducks fell into the Pacific Ocean from a ship. The ducks floated away from the ship. They were caught in currents that took them all over the world. The ducks have been found thousands of miles away from the Pacific. **Oceanographers** tracked them to study the speed of currents.

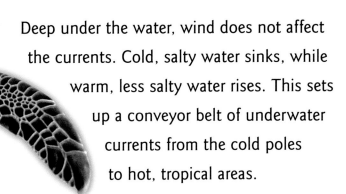

Deep under the water, wind does not affect the currents. Cold, salty water sinks, while warm, less salty water rises. This sets up a conveyor belt of underwater currents from the cold poles to hot, tropical areas.

Currents affect the climate. Cold currents from the poles and warm currents from the **equator** move along coastlines. They change the temperature of land in coastal areas.

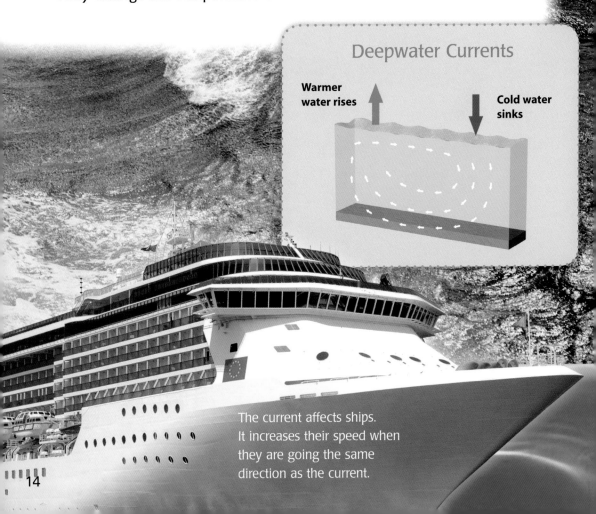

Deepwater Currents

Warmer water rises

Cold water sinks

The current affects ships. It increases their speed when they are going the same direction as the current.

THE WEATHER REPORT

Pacific Problems: El Niño

Sometimes currents cause big trouble. El Niño is the name given to a particular pattern of currents and winds. It appears every three to seven years in the Pacific Ocean.

Normally, the Pacific winds blow from South America to Australia and islands in the western Pacific. This causes the water currents to flow from east to west. This brings much-needed rain to the western Pacific. On the eastern side, near South America, cold water rises to the surface. This brings up nutrients that feed fish.

When El Niño occurs, strong westerly winds reverse the currents. El Niño can cause drought in western Pacific countries. It brings more rain to the east. This can lead to flooding. Fewer fish have been caught in South America during El Niño years.

EL NIÑO CONDITIONS

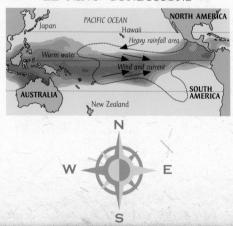

NORMAL CONDITIONS

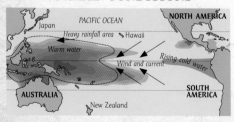

The Gulf Stream is a current. It moves at speeds of 60 to 100 miles a day. It brings warm water from the Caribbean Sea to the North Atlantic Ocean. It is so large and powerful that it can be seen from space!

The Ocean Depths

I wasn't certain what plates had to do with the earth's surface, but I had an idea. Reading on and looking at the diagram helped me confirm my assumptions.

The ocean floor is a landscape much like those we see on land. The only difference is that it is completely under water. There are mountains, plains, and **trenches**. The surface of the earth is made up of plates. These push against each other. The edges of some plates rise up to form mountains. Others are pushed under the surface to form trenches.

The deepest trenches are often close to the edge of a continent. The Mariana Trench is the deepest of all. It's in the Pacific Ocean. It is over 36,000 feet deep! The Atlantic Ocean's deepest trench is the Puerto Rico Trench. This trench is a little over 30,000 feet deep.

Cross Section of Ocean

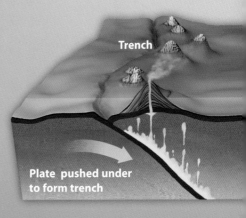

Trench

Plate pushed under to form trench

Ocean Zones

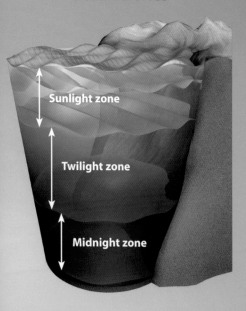

Sunlight zone

Twilight zone

Midnight zone

The depths of the ocean are called the midnight zone. There is no light at all here. The layer above this is called the twilight zone. It is between 1,640 feet and 4,900 feet under water. There is very little light in this zone.

Earth's crust

Mantle

Creatures of the Deep

These deepwater sea creatures live where there is no light at all. They have special organs on their bodies that give off light. These light organs help attract prey.

Hatchet fish

Angler fish

Jellyfish

FIRE AND WATER

Some of the most active volcanoes on the earth are hidden under the oceans. They bring up molten rock from inside the earth. It forms new ocean floor. Cold ocean water leaks down to the heat source. When it is heated, it gushes up through cracks. Water and minerals gush out of the cracks. These cracks are called **hydrothermal vents**.

Hydrothermal Vent

Minerals and hot water

Molten rock and water rise

Molten rock inside the earth

Did You Know?

Vents can be either "black smokers" or "white smokers." This depends on the minerals in the water. Black smokers are named for the dark-colored mineral particles that shoot out. They have more sulfur than white smokers, and are hotter.

MEET THE TUBEWORM

Tubeworms live around hydrothermal vents. In shallow water, they grow to about the size of your hand. But in the deep, deep ocean, they can grow to as long as eight feet!

SHOCKER

A tubeworm has no mouth, intestine, or stomach! To eat, the tubeworm takes in minerals released from hydrothermal vents. Bacteria inside the tubeworm turn those minerals into food.

This is a hard outer covering. It is made of **chitin**. It protects the tubeworm from being eaten. It also filters out toxic chemicals.

The red plume is filled with a kind of blood. If a tubeworm is threatened, it draws in its plume. If the tubeworm is not fast enough, a **predator** may eat the plume.

Tubeworms

Exploring the Deep

How do we know what the deepest, darkest parts of the ocean are like? Some people have explored the ocean depths in the way others have explored space. They have found ways of going there. Or they have sent remote-controlled equipment to take pictures.

In 1942, the first SCUBA equipment was invented. SCUBA stands for Self Contained Underwater Breathing Apparatus. It allows divers to breathe under water. They breathe through a **regulator**. It is connected to an air tank on their back. This equipment can be used to about 100 feet deep. After that, the pressure of the water is too great for human lungs to work. SCUBA led the way for other inventions, such as **submersibles**. These underwater vehicles can explore the ocean floor, even at great depths.

Diver with underwater camera

Words, such as *SCUBA*, that are made up of the beginning letters of other words are called acronyms. Here is another example: *LASER* = Light Amplification by Simulated Emission of Radiation.

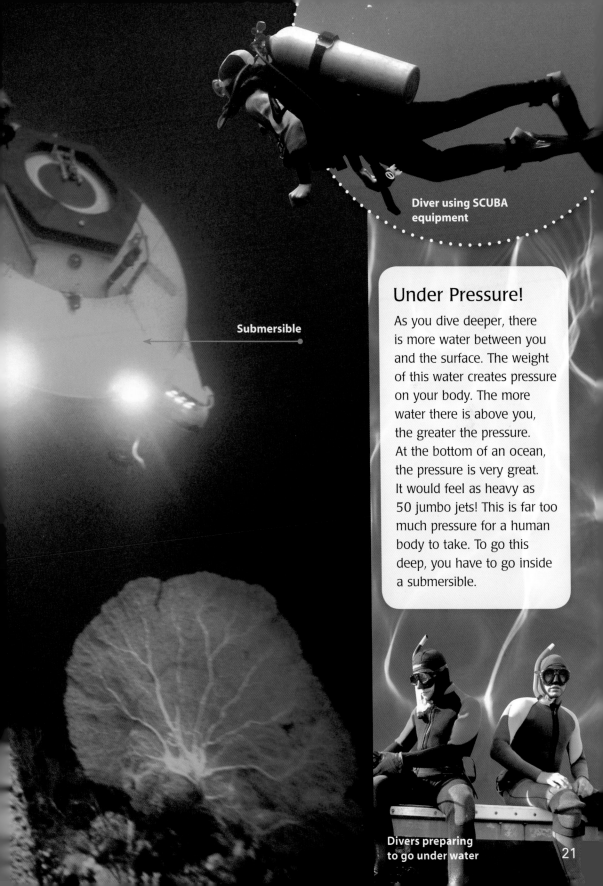

Diver using SCUBA
equipment

Submersible

Under Pressure!

As you dive deeper, there
is more water between you
and the surface. The weight
of this water creates pressure
on your body. The more
water there is above you,
the greater the pressure.
At the bottom of an ocean,
the pressure is very great.
It would feel as heavy as
50 jumbo jets! This is far too
much pressure for a human
body to take. To go this
deep, you have to go inside
a submersible.

Divers preparing
to go under water

Ocean Life

Oceans are the largest **habitats** on earth. They support a huge amount of plant and animal life. Here are some of the living things that make their homes in the ocean.

13,000 different kinds of fish

50,000 different kinds of clams, mussels, and oysters

MEET THE GIANT SQUID

If anything in the sea looks like a monster, it's this incredible creature – the giant squid. It is the world's largest invertebrate. An invertebrate is an animal that has no bones.

SHOCKER

A giant squid has a beak that cuts up its food into small pieces. When a giant squid swallows, the food goes through its brain before it goes into its stomach.

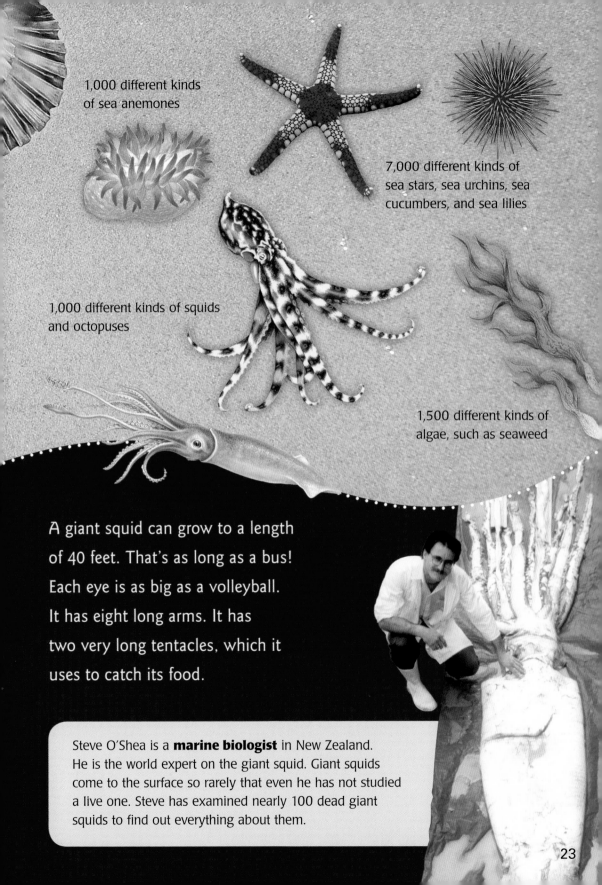

1,000 different kinds of sea anemones

7,000 different kinds of sea stars, sea urchins, sea cucumbers, and sea lilies

1,000 different kinds of squids and octopuses

1,500 different kinds of algae, such as seaweed

A giant squid can grow to a length of 40 feet. That's as long as a bus! Each eye is as big as a volleyball. It has eight long arms. It has two very long tentacles, which it uses to catch its food.

Steve O'Shea is a **marine biologist** in New Zealand. He is the world expert on the giant squid. Giant squids come to the surface so rarely that even he has not studied a live one. Steve has examined nearly 100 dead giant squids to find out everything about them.

Ocean Science

Oceanographers are marine scientists. They study anything and everything to do with the oceans. This includes the rocks, plants, and animals in the oceans. They also look at the currents and landscape.

Did You Know?

The mid-Atlantic ridge was unknown until 1858. It was discovered when the transatlantic telegraph cable was being laid. This cable allowed telegrams, an early form of long-distance communication, to be sent.

Oceanography became an official science in 1872. This was after a famous ship voyage known as the Challenger Expedition. Charles Wyville and John Murray set out from Great Britain on *HMS Challenger*.

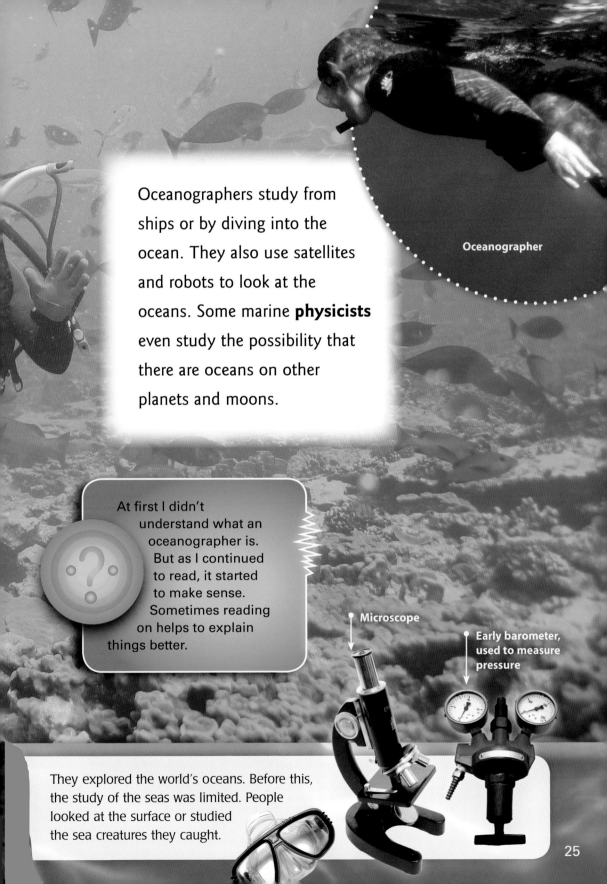

Oceanographers study from ships or by diving into the ocean. They also use satellites and robots to look at the oceans. Some marine **physicists** even study the possibility that there are oceans on other planets and moons.

Oceanographer

At first I didn't understand what an oceanographer is. But as I continued to read, it started to make sense. Sometimes reading on helps to explain things better.

Microscope

Early barometer, used to measure pressure

They explored the world's oceans. Before this, the study of the seas was limited. People looked at the surface or studied the sea creatures they caught.

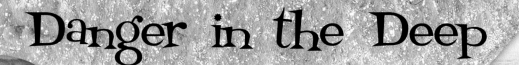

Danger in the Deep

Plastic wrappers and other **debris** can cause great harm to the oceans. Plastic does not break down quickly. Instead it builds up until people clear it away. Marine animals can become tangled in it. Sometimes they eat it, which can harm their digestive systems. Garbage in the ocean can carry **organisms**, such as harmful bacteria, that cause diseases. When the garbage floats from one ocean to another, it can spread diseases as it goes.

When debris is dumped in the ocean:
- animals get tangled in it
- animals eat it and are harmed by it
- it can spread diseases around the oceans

Scientists have discovered a new **parasite**. It destroys krill. Krill are small animals that whales eat. The parasite gets into a krill and eats its organs. The parasite multiplies inside the krill. Then the krill explodes! The parasites burst out and look for new victims.

Ship Problems

Ships carry tanks of water for **ballast**. Sometimes ships fill their tanks in one ocean and empty them in another. Bacteria, animals, and plants can end up in new waters. Moving things to new places like this can threaten the plants and animals that are already there.

Danger!

A floating grocery bag looks like a jellyfish to some animals. Swallowing a plastic bag can cause an animal to suffocate.

Radioactive Threat

Radioactive chemicals are very dangerous. Nuclear reactions inside a power station are contained, but radioactive waste is produced. It is very difficult to get rid of the waste safely.

If radioactive waste gets into the oceans, it causes damage to animals and plants. Fish are born with **deformities** that can kill them. If it gets into the human **food chain**, it can cause cancer in people. The water cycle turns the ocean water into rain. This means that some radioactive waste can get into drinking water. It can also get into the plants that people and animals eat.

Did You Know?
There are old test sites for nuclear weapons near the Arctic Ocean. This has led to grave concerns about radioactive contamination of the Arctic.

Radioactive chemicals are very dangerous. They:
- damage plants and animals
- can cause deformities
- can cause cancer

Science to the Rescue

Ashanti Pyrtle: Oceanographer

Ashanti Pyrtle is an oceanographer at the University of South Florida. She studies what happens to the radioactive waste that gets into oceans and rivers.

Radioactive waste leaks into marine systems from nuclear power-plant disasters, or as the "fallout" from nuclear weapon testing.

Ashanti looks at how the radioactive atoms that make up the waste are carried around the oceans. Her research might help scientists predict how waste spreads after an accident. It might also help them find new ways to clean up radioactive waste.

Radiation warning sign

Out of Fish!

Can you imagine a world where fish isn't on the menu anywhere? It's not just an idea. It's a reality if the problems of **commercial** fishing are not solved.

Fishing has provided food for many of the world's people for thousands of years. However, the oceans have now been overfished. More and more fish have been caught, including smaller and younger fish that have not had time to breed. This means that fish populations are getting smaller. If we keep catching fish in large numbers, many species will become **extinct**.

Aquaculture

Aquaculture is a name for fish farming. Fish are bred in enclosed areas of the sea. These "farms" often have problems, such as disease. Aquaculture has to be planned carefully to be successful.

If nothing is done within the next ten years, you will not find fish on any menu or in any stores. Fish sticks and tuna sandwiches will be things of the past.

Trawling the Bottom

To catch as many fish as they can, some fishermen use huge nets that scrape the seabed. This means that they catch younger and rarer fish. This makes the problems worse.

Fishing boat with trawling net

People are learning that there are no longer enough fish in the sea. Fish populations are dropping. This affects the entire food chain. The oceans need protection. Banning commercial fishing to allow fish populations to recover is one way to do this. However, fish are an important source of food for many people.

WHAT DO YOU THINK?

Should commercial fishing be banned completely, even if it means that people will lose their food and income?

PRO

I think that fishing should be completely stopped for a few years. People can eat plants and other animals too. That way the fish populations could recover. Then we could begin fishing carefully so the problems don't start again. If we don't, there will be greater problems in the future. My grandchildren won't know what a fish is!

Fishing is also a vital source of income. For many families around the world, fishing is a skill that has been passed down through the generations. If commercial fishing were banned, many people would be out of work. There would be a shortage of food. But if nothing changes, there will be no fish left to catch.

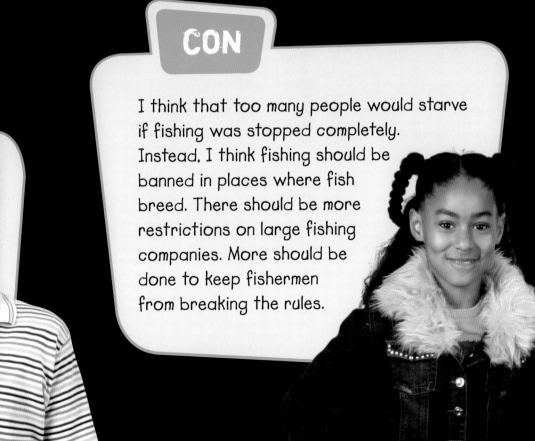

CON

I think that too many people would starve if fishing was stopped completely. Instead, I think fishing should be banned in places where fish breed. There should be more restrictions on large fishing companies. More should be done to keep fishermen from breaking the rules.

GLOSSARY

ballast (*BAL uhst*) something heavy, such as water or sand, that is carried by a ship to make it more stable

chitin a hard, protective material that forms part of the shell or outer skeleton of animals such as tubeworms, crabs, and insects

commercial to do with buying or selling

condense to change from a vapor, or gas, into a liquid

continent one of the seven large land masses on Earth, such as Asia or North America

current the movement of water in a river or an ocean

deformity an unusually shaped body part

ebb the movement of the tide back out to sea

equator an imaginary line around the middle of the earth, halfway between the North and South poles

extinct (*ek STINGKT*) died out completely

flow to move along smoothly

food chain a pathway linking a plant and several animals in which each one feeds on the one before it

gravity the force that pulls things toward the center of the earth

habitat an area where a plant or an animal lives naturally

marine biologist a scientist who studies plants and animals in the oceans

parasite an animal that lives on or in another animal and feeds on it

physicist (*FIZZ uh sist*) a scientist who studies energy and matter

predator an animal that hunts and eats other animals

regulator a SCUBA device that controls the air from a diver's tank so that he or she can breathe under water

Regulator

FIND OUT MORE

BOOKS

Burns, Loree Griffin. *Tracking Trash: Flotsam, Jetsam, and the Science of Ocean Motion*. Houghton Mifflin, 2007.

Hall, Kirsten. *Deep Sea Adventures*. Children's Press, 2004.

Ocean Life. Time-Life Books, 2000.

Schmauss, Judy Kentor. *Wicked and Wonderful Water*. Scholastic Inc., 2008.

Stille, Darlene R. *Oceans*. Children's Press, 2000.

Taylor, Barbara. *Rivers and Oceans*. Kingfisher, 2002.

WEB SITES

Go to the Web sites below to learn more about ocean life.

www.oceanicresearch.org/lesson.html

www.water-ed.org/kids.asp

www.calstatela.edu/faculty/eviau/edit557/oceans

www.montereyaquarium.org/lc

INDEX

ABOUT THE AUTHOR

Judy Kentor Schmauss has written many fiction and nonfiction books for children. Water has always been a fascination for her, so writing about it was right up her alley. The idea that we're drinking the same water that the dinosaurs drank knocks her socks off! Judy loves the animals that live in the ocean, especially octopuses. If there's an aquarium in a city she visits, you know she'll be there.